Living Things

Wendy Madgwick

WAYLAND

Titles in this series:
Up in the Air • Water Play • Magnets and Sparks
Super Sound • Super Materials • Light and Dark
Living Things • On the Move

First published in 1998 by
Wayland Publishers Ltd.
61 Western Road, Hove,
East Sussex BN3 1JD, England

Find Wayland on the Internet at http://www.wayland.co.uk

Series devised by
Tucker Slingsby Ltd
Berkeley House
73 Upper Richmond Road
London SW15 2SZ

Designer: Anita Ruddell
Illustrations: Catherine
Ward/Simon Girling
Associates
Photographer: Andrew
Sydenham

Picture Acknowledgements: pages 5, 10, 20 top, 23
Bruce Coleman /K. Taylor; page 8 top Bruce Coleman/H.
Reinhard; page 8 bottom Bruce Coleman/G. Dore; page
12 Trip/J. Gilbert; page 17 OSF/K. Sandved; page 20
bottom Bruce Coleman/J. Rydell; page 22 Bruce
Coleman/J. Burton; page 24 Bruce Coleman/G. Ziesler.

Many thanks to JD, Kondwani, Liuzayani, Poppy and
Shinnosuke.

Words that appear in **bold** in the text are explained in the
glossary on page 30.

British Library Cataloguing in Publication Data
Madgwick, Wendy
Living Things. – (Science Starters). – Juvenile literature
I. Title II. Ward, Catherine
578

ISBN 0 7502 2166 6

Colour reproduction by Page Turn,
England
Printed and bound in Italy by G. Canale
& C.S.p.A., Turin

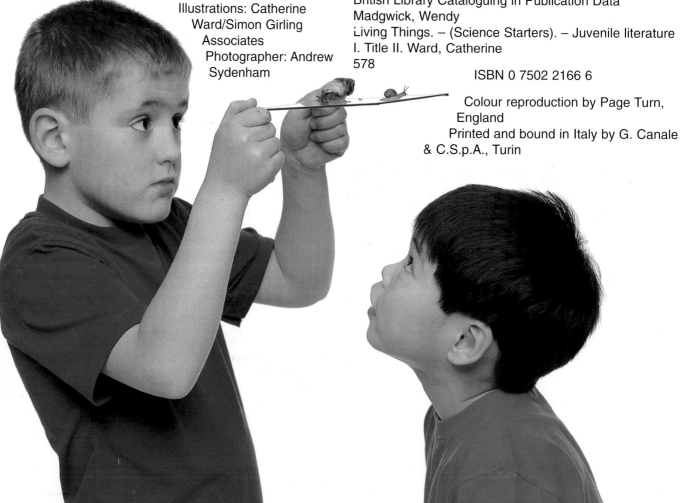

Contents

Looking at living things

Living things come in all shapes and sizes. This book looks at some plants and animals to see how they live.

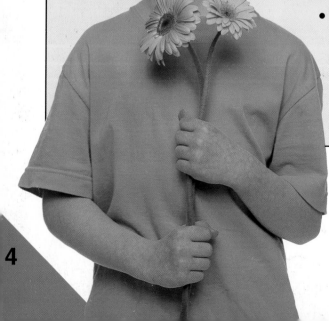

• Tell a grown-up what you are doing. Ask him or her if you can do the activity. You may need to ask him or her to help with some of the activities.

• Always read through the activity before you start.

• Collect all the materials you will need and put them on a tray. They are listed on page 28.

• Make sure you have enough space to set up your activity.

• Be careful when you collect small animals. Do not hurt them. Do not keep them for more than two days. Always put them back where you found them.

• Watch what happens carefully.

• Keep a notebook. Draw pictures or write down what you did and what happened.

• Always clear up when you have finished. Wash your hands.

► This bee is attracted by the colour and smell of the flower. Find out how to puzzle a bee with your own flower on page 11.

4

What is life?

Objects in the world can be put into two groups – living and non-living. Living things come in all shapes and sizes, but they all take in 'food'. This helps them grow, have babies and respond to the world around them.

Alive or not?

Look at this picture. Which things are alive and which are not?

The plastic brick, stone, salt, glass, cup and straws are not alive. The girl, dog, plant, worms and spider are alive. The apple was alive before it was picked!

Rock animals

Rocks are not alive but they can make good toy animals. Let's make one.

1 Choose a smooth oval stone and wash it well.

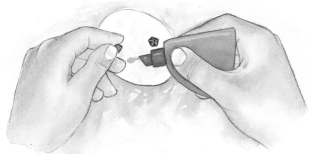

2 Glue two small beads at one end of the stone for eyes.

3 Cut out two ear shapes from paper. Glue them to the head.

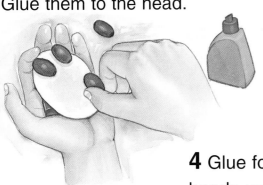

4 Glue four large beads underneath the stone as legs.

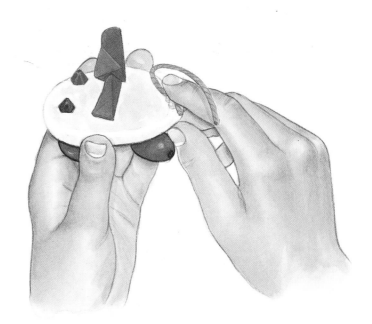

5 Glue a piece of wool to the back end as a tail. See how many different kinds of animal you can make.

7

Going green

Plants do not eat as you do. They make their food from sunlight, water and carbon dioxide gas. This is called **photosynthesis**.

▶▲ Trees are plants. They cannot move around, but they are alive. Trees can live for hundreds of years.

▶ Mosses and ferns are plants that do not have flowers.

Plenty of plants

These plants look different but they all have the same parts. Plants have roots to anchor them in the ground. They are supported by stems and their green leaves make food. Dig up a weed and look for these parts.

Thirsty plants

If you do not water most plants they will die. Find out how much water a plant sucks up.

1 Cover a jar of water with cling film. Make a hole in the cling film. Push a plant into the water. Mark the water level with a felt-tipped pen.

3 The water level should be lower. You should see water drops on the inside of the plastic bag.

The water has risen up the plant stem into the leaves. **Water vapour** lost through the leaves has cooled on the plastic bag. It has formed drops of water.

2 Put a large plastic bag over the plant. Tie it in place with string. Leave the plant for a few days.

Flower power

Flowers come in all shapes, sizes and colours. They contain male **pollen** cells and female **ovules** or egg cells.

petal

stigma

anther

▲ Bees visit flowers to drink the **nectar**. They take pollen from one flower to another. Pollen looks like a yellow powder. Sometimes pollen is spread by the wind.

Pretty flowers

Look at this lily. The pale pink parts are the **petals**. Pollen is made by the **anthers**. Pollen from other lilies is collected on the **stigma**. This is in the middle of the flower.

False flowers

Make a paper flower and see if bees will visit it.

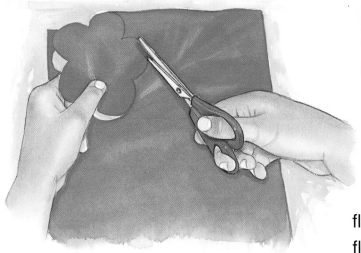

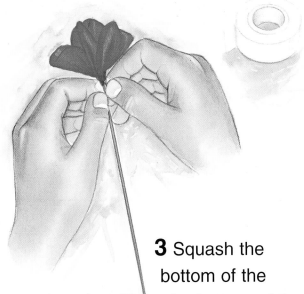

1 Cut out a flower shape from brightly coloured tissue paper.

3 Squash the bottom of the flower together. Tape the bottom of the flower to the wire.

2 Push a piece of thin wire through the middle of the flower.

4 Sprinkle a drop of perfume on the flower.

Put your paper flower outside with some other flowers. Watch and see if bees visit your flower.

A bee may be fooled by your flower. Bees are attracted to flowers by the smell and colour.

Fruits and seeds

When a male pollen cell joins with an ovule, a **seed** is formed. Seeds grow in **fruits**. Fruits can be hard like acorns or soft like tomatoes.

◀ This is part of a conifer tree. It has **cones** instead of flowers. Seeds grow inside each cone.

Look at these fruits. Can you see the seeds? Cut an apple through the middle. Count the seeds inside. Draw the apple and its seeds. Collect some more fruits and look at their seeds.

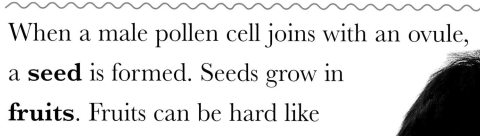

Fly away

Plants cannot move around, so they spread their seeds in other ways.

1 Collect three sycamore seeds. Leave one seed whole. Cut off one wing from a second seed. Cut off both wings from the last seed.

2 Go outside with a friend on a fairly windy day. Hold the seeds at the same height. Twirl them round and let them go.

Which seed spins the best? Which one travels furthest? Why do sycamore seeds have wings?

The seed with both wings spins best and travels furthest. The wings on sycamore seeds help them travel away from the parent tree. Can you think of other ways in which seeds are spread?

Get growing

A seed can grow into a new plant. What does a seed need to **germinate** and grow? Let's find out.

Cress head

1 Put four empty egg shells in egg cups. Fill one with potting compost. Fill the other three with cotton wool.

2 Sprinkle some cress seeds on the top of each one.

3 Gently water three egg shells. Leave one with cotton wool dry.

4 Put the shells on a window sill. Put an empty tin over one shell filled with wet cotton wool. No sunlight will reach these seeds. Check your seeds every day. Gently water the wet ones if they feel dry.

5 Look at them after about a week. Which seeds have grown? Which seeds look green and healthy? Which seeds have grown most? Make a chart of what you find.

The seeds without water should not have grown. Those without sunlight should look unhealthy and pale. Those grown in the sunlight should be green and healthy. The seeds grown in potting compost should have grown most. Cress seeds need sunlight, water and food to grow well.

wet compost

wet cotton wool

wet cotton wool and no sunlight

dry cotton wool

No legs

Animals come in all shapes and sizes. Most animals can move, but they don't all have legs.

One foot

Carefully collect a snail from the garden. Put the snail on a piece of glass. Look at its shell. Look at its soft body and head with four **tentacles**.

Watch how the snail moves. Can you see a slimy trail?

The snail moves on a big muscle called its foot. Ripples pass down the foot from front to back. These carry the snail along. The slime helps the snail move easily.

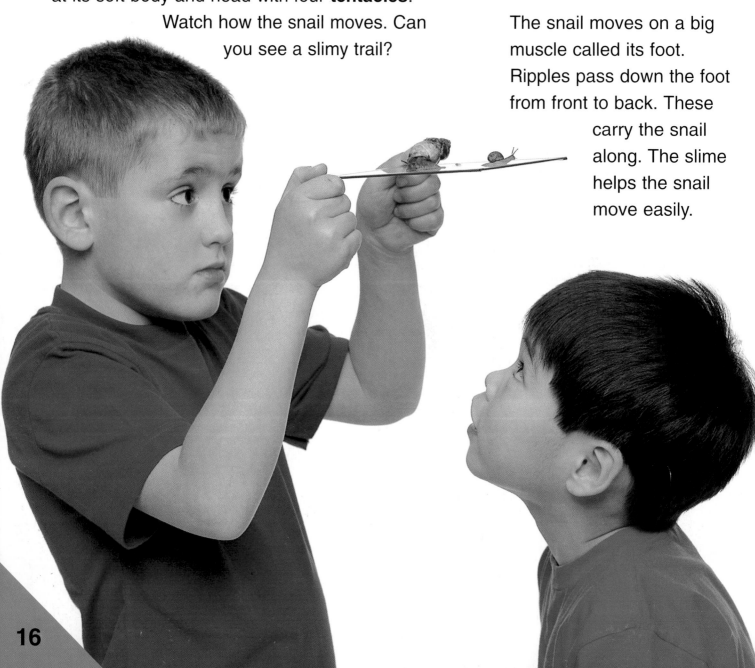

Wriggle along

Carefully collect an earthworm from the garden. Place it on a wooden board or a piece of stiff paper. Gently feel its soft body. Watch it move.

The earthworm moves by changing its shape. It grips the ground with its back end and pushes forward its front end. It becomes long and thin. It then grips with its front end and pulls its back end forwards. The worm becomes short and fat.

▲ A squid uses a jet of water to push itself through the water.

Legs, legs, legs

We walk on two legs. Cats and dogs have four legs. Many other animals have more legs.

Creepy crawlies

Carefully collect some small creatures like those in the photograph. Ask a grown-up to help you. Look at the animals and draw them. Count their legs. Put the animals back where you found them.

Beetles, flies and bees are insects with six legs. Spiders have eight legs. Woodlice have 14 legs. A centipede has between 30 and 354 legs. A worm has no legs.

Active ants

You can watch how ants live by making an antery.

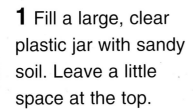

1 Fill a large, clear plastic jar with sandy soil. Leave a little space at the top.

3 Make a small hole in the soil. Put the eggs and ants in the hole. Cover the jar with fine net. Leave the ants for several days. Watch what happens.

Ants live together in a **colony**. They make a nest of tunnels in the soil. There are different kinds of ants. The queen ant lays eggs. Worker ants gather food, guard the colony and look after the eggs and the queen.

2 Carefully collect some black ants and their eggs from an ants' **nest**. Ask a grown-up to help you.

Lights out

Some animals like to live in the light. Others prefer to live in dark places.

▲ Dragonflies hunt in the day. Their huge eyes help them spot a tasty meal.

▲ Bats live in dark caves and buildings in the daytime. At night they come out to feed.

Dark or light?

1 Put a layer of damp soil in three large, clear plastic boxes. Collect some woodlice, spiders and centipedes.

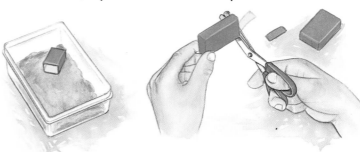

2 Cut a side out of three small cardboard boxes. Put one of these dens in each box.

3 Put woodlice in one box, centipedes in the second and spiders in the third. Cover the boxes with cling film. Make several tiny holes in the cling film.

Woodlice like damp, dark places. They will spend most of their time in the dark den.

Centipedes live in dark places. They hunt at night. They spend more time in the dark than the light.

Spiders are hunters. Some hide in dark places. Many spend time hunting in the light.

4 Keep the animals for a day or two. Check them three or four times a day. Count the numbers in the light and dark. Keep a record of what you find. Which animal spends most time in the dark?

These children are watching how the animals behave. Remember, the animals need soil if they are kept for a few hours.

All change

All living things produce young. Some animals change a lot as they grow up. The babies look completely different from the adults. Others look like little adults.

Water babies

Look at this picture. Can you see the eggs wrapped in jelly? They are frog's eggs. Can you see the tiny black animals swimming around? They are baby frogs called **tadpoles**. They live in water. Soon they will grow legs, lose their tails and hop on to land.

▼ Kittens look a lot like adult cats.

► Adult frogs live on land and in the water. They have short bodies and no tails. They have small front legs and strong back legs for jumping.

Jump!

1 Draw and colour a large frog shape (you can trace this one). Cut it out. Make another one, but colour the opposite side this time.

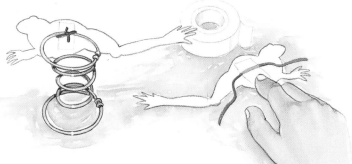

2 Tape a piece of wool to the back of each frog. Tie one to each side of a spring.

3 Press the spring down and let it go. Watch your frog hop.

23

On the wing

Some animals like birds and butterflies move by flying. They fly using wings.

▶ Look at these birds flying.
What covers their bodies and wings?
How do their wings move as they fly?
Where are their legs and feet?

A bird's body is covered by feathers.
The wings move up and down as they fly.
Their legs and feet are tucked under their body out of the way.

Flutter by
Make a fluttering butterfly.

2 Fold up the bottom edge as shown.

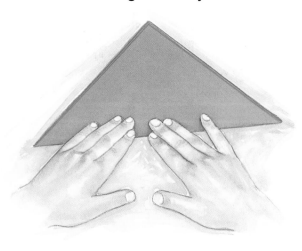

1 Take a square of thin card. Fold two corners together to make a triangle.

3 Fold the paper in half from side to side. Make sure the edges meet.

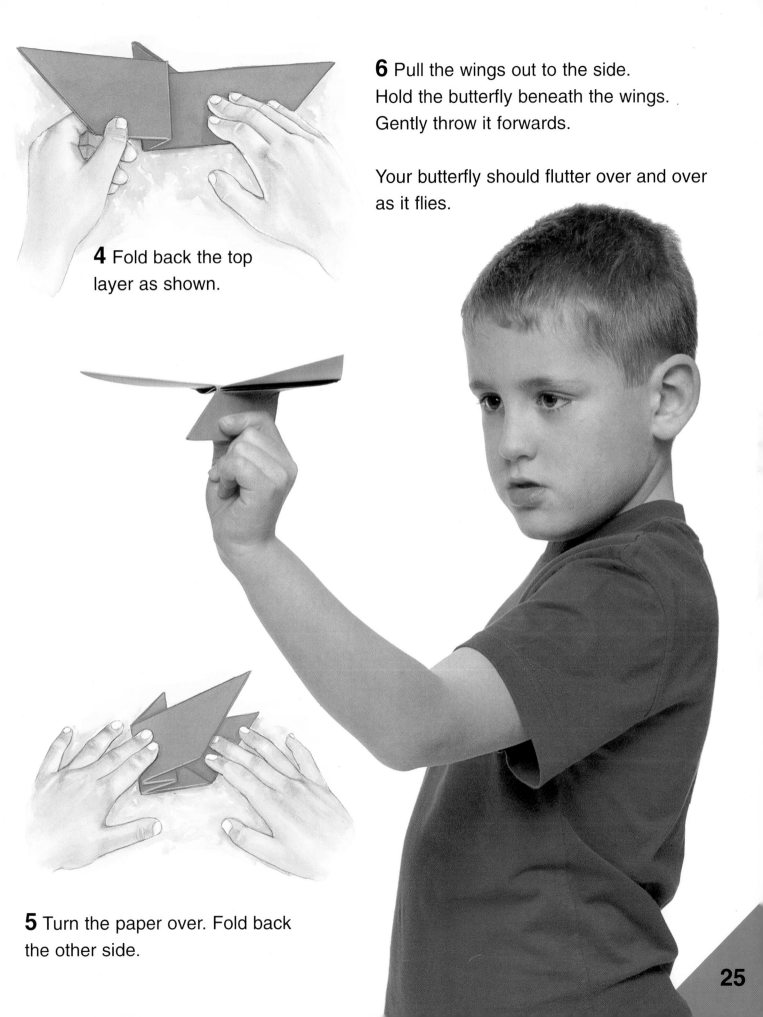

4 Fold back the top layer as shown.

5 Turn the paper over. Fold back the other side.

6 Pull the wings out to the side. Hold the butterfly beneath the wings. Gently throw it forwards.

Your butterfly should flutter over and over as it flies.

You too

Humans are animals too. People come in all shapes and sizes. What you look like depends on your parents and where you live.

Move and bend

You can move and bend easily because you have joints. Try making this jointed puppet.

1 Cut out and colour body, leg and arm shapes from thin card. Draw on the crosses as shown.

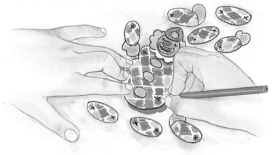

2 With a sharp pencil, make a hole in the card through the crosses.

3 Use paper fasteners to join the leg pieces together. Do the same with the arms. Join the legs and arms to the body.

4 Tape some thin string to the head and hands.

5 Tie the other ends of the string to a thin stick. Make your puppet move.

Roller or not?

Look at your friends. In what ways are they the same as you? How are they different from you? Sometimes differences are hidden. Ask your friends if they can roll their tongues into a tube. How many are rollers? How many are non-rollers?

Materials you will need

p. 6 What is life? – small oval stones, water, small and large beads, wool, strong glue, paper, round-ended scissors, felt-tipped pens.

p.8 Going green – a weed to look at, jar, water, cling film, sharp pencil to make a hole in the cling film, plastic bag, plant with roots, felt-tipped pens, string.

p. 10 Flower power – brightly coloured tissue paper, round-ended scissors, thin wire, sticky tape, perfume.

p. 12 Fruits and seeds – apple and other fruits such as a tomato, broad bean, acorn. Ask a grown-up to cut the fruits. Three sycamore seeds, round-ended scissors. Ask a friend to help.

p.14 Get growing – four empty, clean egg shells, four egg cups, cotton wool, potting compost or soil, water, teaspoon, mustard cress seeds, small box or tin to cover one egg shell, pencil, paper.

p. 16 No legs – snail, piece of glass, wooden board or a piece of stiff paper, small trowel to collect an earthworm; you might need the help of a grown-up.

p. 18 Legs, legs, legs – small clear plastic containers, a small spade to help you collect beetles, woodlice, flies and centipedes, paper, pencil. To make the antery you will need a large, clear plastic box or jar, sandy soil (mix ordinary soil with sand to make a light sandy soil), fine net, black ants and ant eggs. Ask a grown-up to help you collect the animals.

p. 20 Lights out – clear plastic boxes, damp soil, some woodlice, spiders and centipedes, cling film, three small cardboard boxes, sharp pencil or cocktail stick to make holes in the cling film.

p. 22 All change – paper, coloured pencils, round-ended scissors, wool, sticky tape, small metal spring.

p. 24 On the wing – square of thin card.

p. 26 You too – friends to help you, thin white card, sharp pencil, coloured pencils, paper fasteners, round-ended scissors, thin string, sticky tape, thin stick.

Hints to helpers

Pages 6 and 7

Talk about what makes things living or non-living, e.g. whether they can grow, move, have young, respond to what is going on around them. Ask the children to think about the main differences between plants and animals. Discuss why the apple is no longer living and what will happen to it after a while.

As the children make the rock animals, talk about what they could put on their animals to make them like real animals. Discuss what each part is used for, e.g. eyes for seeing, ears for hearing, nose for smelling, mouth for eating and making a noise, legs for moving. Compare them with the senses the children have and how they use them in everyday life.

Pages 8 and 9

Talk about green plants and why animals need plants to live. Explain why it is important not to cut down too many forests. Talk about the different kinds of green plant. Look at the different parts of a flowering plant and discuss what each part is used for. Discuss the conditions plants need to grow well.

Pages 10 and 11

Discuss why some plants have flowers. Most flowers contain the male and female parts of a plant which make new plants. Explain how some flowers attract bees and other animals to land on them. The animals then spread the pollen to other flowers. Discuss other ways the pollen could be spread, e.g. by the wind. Explain why plants need to make so much pollen, e.g. some animals feed on pollen grains, wind blows pollen around, so a lot of it is lost.

Pages 12 and 13

Talk about why plants make seeds and why the seeds need to be spread away from the parent plant. This is linked with what a plant needs to grow well. Mention that if plants are crowded together they may not get enough water and light etc. Discuss the different ways seeds can be taken from one place to another, e.g. very light seeds can be blown by the wind, sticky seeds can get stuck to the fur or feet of animals.

Pages 14 and 15

Talk about why plants make new plants and why gardeners and farmers use seeds to grow food. Discuss the different things a seed needs in order to germinate and develop into a healthy plant. Explain why farmers and gardeners need to water and feed plants to help them grow. Lead on to what happens to plants if there is a drought or if the seedlings grow in places where there is little sunlight, water or food.

Pages 16 and 17

Ask the children to think of as many different kinds of animal as they can. Talk about the different kinds of animals and compare their shapes to people's shapes. Talk about the different ways animals move and why they need to move, e.g looking for a safe place to rest, hunting for food. Discuss what the snail uses its shell for, e.g. to protect its soft body, to stop it from drying out. Talk about what snails eat and why they have tentacles. Look at the worms and talk about why they can live in the earth and wriggle through the soil.

Talk about why we need to care for all animals, even tiny ones. Discuss where snails and worms are found and why we should always return them to the places they were found.

Pages 18 and 19

Explain that we need to take great care not to hurt small animals when picking them up. It is better to use a spoon or trowel to pick them up rather than your fingers. This will stop the animals from being damaged as well as protecting you. Explain that the children should never try to pick up a wasp or bee as they may sting and this could be dangerous.

Always collect black garden ants, not red ones as these can 'sting' and cause a rash. Ant nests can usually be found in fairly sheltered places near or under stones or plants. The entrance to the nest is often a round hole and a stream of ants is usually going in and out. The oval, cream-coloured eggs are about the size of a small grain of rice. Great care should be taken in picking up some ants and eggs. You should make sure that you collect several ants for each egg. The soil should contain bits of food for the ants, but you could put some bits of bread and grains of sugar on the top of the soil as extra food. Make sure the ants and eggs are returned to a suitable place when the children have watched them for a week or so.

Pages 20 and 21

Talk about why different animals live in different places, e.g. fish live in water, birds fly in the sky and nest in trees, worms live in the soil, etc. Discuss why some animals prefer damp, dark places and others like light, open places. Make sure that the children take great care when they collect the animals. Only keep them for a day or two at the most, then return them to the place where they were found.

Pages 22 and 23

Talk about why animals have young and the different kind of young that various animals have. Talk about how some animals, such as frogs, change their shape and where they live as they grow up. Talk about the shape of the tadpole and how it is best suited for a life in the water. Then look at the adult frog and discuss how its big back legs and strong muscles help it to jump on land and swim through the water. Talk about how it uses its legs like a spring to push off from the ground and leap along. Discuss how the young of insects change, e.g caterpillars, chrysalis and butterflies. Link this to how people change as they grow up.

Pages 24 and 25

Talk about the different kinds of flying animals – insects, bats and birds. Discuss the things they have in common – wings, light bodies etc. Discuss the different ways they fly, how they use their wings and what they do with their wings when they're not flying.

Pages 26 and 27

Talk about the fact that people are animals too and that they are similar in some ways to wild animals. Using the puppet, discuss how people move, talk and use their senses to help them live. Encourage the children to think about how they are the same as their friends and in what ways they are different, e.g. size, hair and eye colour, likes and dislikes in food.

Glossary

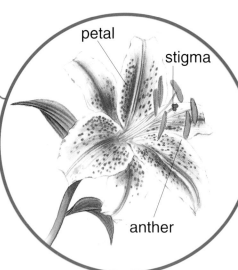

petal

stigma

anther

Anthers The parts of a flower that make pollen.

Colony A group of animals that live together.

Cones The parts of a conifer tree that contain the male or female 'cells'. Seeds grow inside the female cone.

Fruits The parts of a flowering plant that contain the seeds.

Germinate When a seed starts to grow into a new plant.

Nectar A sweet, sugary liquid made by flowers.

Nest A special place made and lived in by an animal. Some animals lay their eggs or bring up their babies in a nest.

Ovules The female 'cells' of a plant that can grow into a seed.

Petals The brightly coloured parts of a flower that attract bees.

Photosynthesis The way in which green plants make food. They make sugar from water and carbon dioxide gas using energy from sunlight.

Pollen Tiny yellow grains made by a flower or cone. They contain the male 'cells' of the plant.

Seed The tiny part of a plant formed when female and male 'cells' join together. A seed can grow into a new plant.

Stigma The female part of a flower that collects the pollen grains.

Tadpoles Young frogs. A tadpole has a head and a tail but no legs. The legs grow as the tadpole gets bigger.

Tentacles Long, thin finger-like parts on the bodies of animals such as snails. They are used for feeling and seeing.

Water vapour Very tiny droplets of water in the air. They are often too small for you to see.

Further reading

Autumn, Spring, Summer, Winter all by Gabrielle Woolfitt, Science Through The Seasons. 1995; Wayland Publishers, Hove.

Butterflies and Moths by Barrie Watts, Keeping Minibeasts. 1991; Franklin Watts, London.

Earthworms by Chris Hellwood, Keeping Minibeasts. 1991; Franklin Watts, London.

Flowers, Minibeasts, Trees all by Henry Pluckrose, Walkabout. 1993; Franklin Watts, London.

Minibeast by Paul Wright, Handmade Habitats. 1992; A&C Black, London.

Index